THE DEMI-GODS OF GREEK MYTHOLOGY

Mythology 4th Grade
Children's Greek & Roman Books

Speedy Publishing LLC
40 E. Main St. #1156
Newark, DE 19711
www.speedypublishing.com
Copyright 2017

All Rights reserved. No part of this book may be reproduced or used in any way or form or by any means whether electronic or mechanical, this means that you cannot record or photocopy any material ideas or tips that are provided in this book.

A demi-god is someone with a human parent and a divine parent. The divine parent did not have to be a major Olympian god, but might be one of lesser power, including a nymph. They were believed to have unique abilities beyond that of a mere mortal.

Many were considered to be heroes in several different ways. Their stories have inspired countless generations of historical societies and figures. In this book, we will be learning about some of these demigods of Greek mythology and who they were.

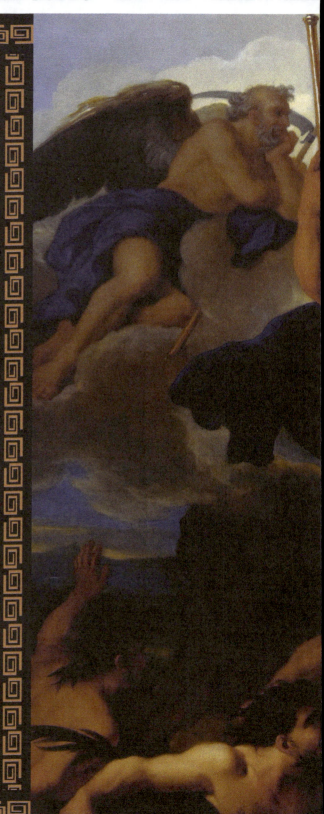

Homer

FAMOUS DEMIGODS

There are several legends and myths that surround these Greek demigods. A few of the more famous stories were documented in the Iliad and the Odyssey, by Homer, a Greek writer. The more well-known demigods were Hercules, Perseus, Achilles and Helen of Troy, a female demigod.

THE ILIAD

This is a classic poem written by Homer, telling the story about the final year of the Trojan War that was fought between the Greeks and the City of Troy.

Hercules Statue

HERCULES

Hercules was referred to as the greatest of these mythological Greek heroes, being known for his intelligence, courage and incredible strength. While his actual Roman name is Hercules, the Greeks referred to him as Heracles.

HIS EARLY YEARS

Zeus, king of the gods, was his father and Alcmene, a gorgeous human princess, was his mother.

Statue of Zeus

Infant Hercules Strangling the Serpent

Hercules was always quite strong, even as a baby. Once Zeus' wife, the goddess Hera, found out about this child Hercules, she wanted him dead, and snuck two big snakes inside his crib. Baby Hercules, however, was able to grab the snakes by their necks and strangled both of them with only his bare hands!

GROWING UP

Alcmene, his mother, attempted to raise him similar to a typical kid. One day, however, he was mad at his music teacher and hit him on the head with a lyre, killing him by accident.

He liked the outdoors and went to live in the hills, working a cattle herder. When he was 18 years old, a large lion attacked his cattle herd and he killed it with his bare hands.

HERCULES IS TRICKED

Hercules proceeded to marry a princess by the name of Megara and they lived a happy life with their family. This angered the goddess Hera and she then tricked him into believing that his family was a bunch of snakes. He killed the snakes and then realized he had killed his family. He became quite sad and guilt-ridden.

Megara Statue

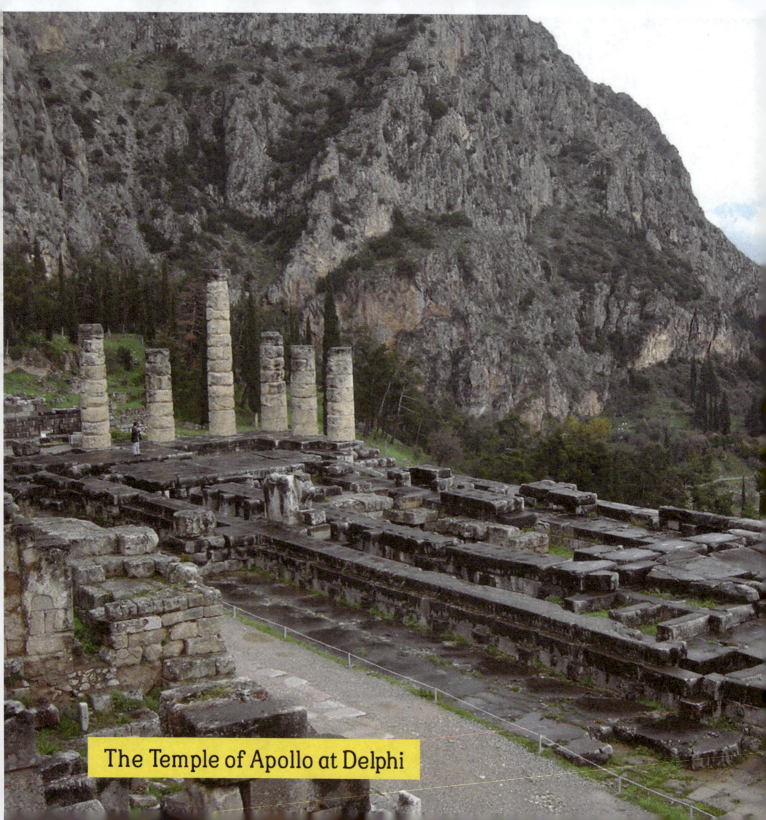
The Temple of Apollo at Delphi

ORACLE OF DELPHI

He decided he had to get rid of this guilty feeling and went to the Oracle of Delphi for advice. The Oracle advised him that he had to serve King Eurystheus for ten years and do each task the king asked him to do. He would then be forgiven and not feel guilty any more. These tasks became known as the Twelve Labors of Hercules.

Not only did he use his courage and strength to accomplish this, he also used intelligence, in order to accomplish these Twelve Labors.

Hercules Sarcophagus Depicting the Twelve Labors of Hercules

Perseus Riding Pegasus

PERSEUS

Perseus' parents were a human female named Danae and his father was Zeus. He possessed both intelligence and strength. His most well-known exploit was slaying Medusa, a monster that had writhing snakes for her hair and was so repugnant to look at that it would take only once glance to turn someone to stone.

Being the son of Zeus, he received a lot of assistance from the gods: Hermes provided him with winged sandals so he could fly, Zeus provided him with a sword, Hades provided him with a cloak of invisibility, and Athena provided him with a polished shield. He was able to use the shield to view the reflection of the monster and avoid directly gazing on her. He defeated Medusa by chopping her head off.

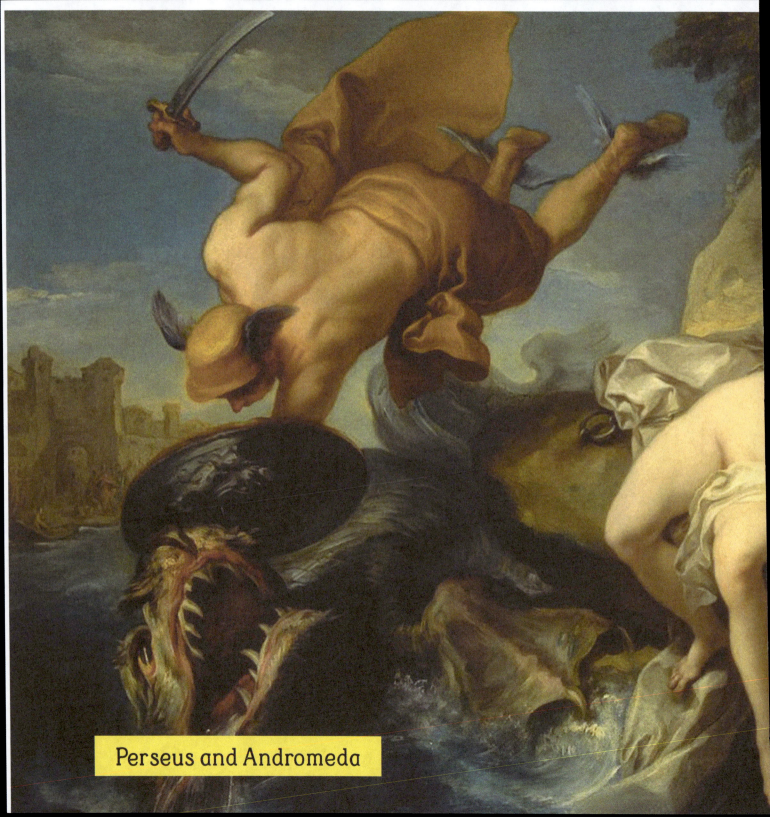

Perseus and Andromeda

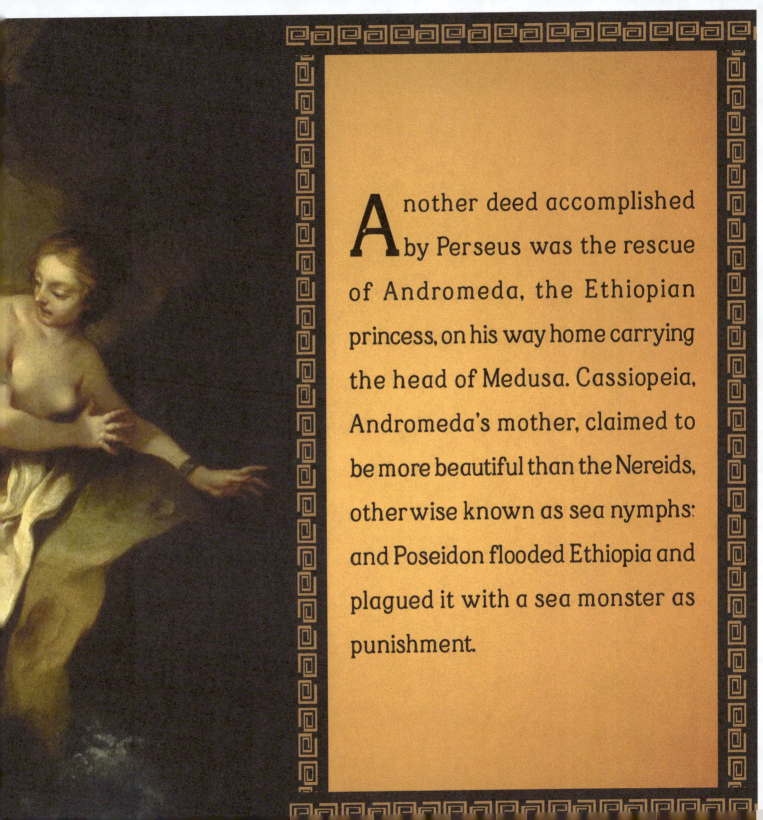

Another deed accomplished by Perseus was the rescue of Andromeda, the Ethiopian princess, on his way home carrying the head of Medusa. Cassiopeia, Andromeda's mother, claimed to be more beautiful than the Nereids, otherwise known as sea nymphs: and Poseidon flooded Ethiopia and plagued it with a sea monster as punishment.

King Cepheus, who as Andromeda's father, was informed by an oracle that he would put a stop to the ills if he would expose Andromeda to this monster, which he proceeded to accomplish. As Perseus was passing by, he saw the princess and fell in love. He was able to turn the monster to stone by showing Medusa's head to it. He then went on to marry Andromeda.

Perseus and Andromeda

He would then accompany his mother back to Argos, where he struck her father, Acrisius, accidently as he was throwing a discus, which killed him, which fulfilled the prophecy that he would kill his grandfather. He left Argos and founded Mycenae to be his capital, and he became the ancestor of Perseids, which included Hercules. His legend has been a favorite subject in sculpture and painting, both ancient as well as Renaissance. The key characters in this legend, Andromeda, Cassiopeia, Cepheus, Perseus, and the sea monster (Cetus), all are part of the night sky as constellations.

ACHILLES

He was known to be one of the greatest heroes and warrior of Greek Mythology and was a key character in the Iliad by Homer, where he fought during the Trojan War against Troy.

Achilles

BIRTH OF ACHILLES

His father was the king of the Myrmidons, Peleus, and Thetis, a sea nymph, was his mother. Once he was born, Thetis wanted to protect him from harm's way. She held him by his heel and dunked him in the river Styx. According to Greek Mythology, the river Styx was in the Underworld and held special powers. Achilles then became invulnerable everywhere except at his heel, where Thetis had held him.

Since he was a half-god, he was quite strong and would become a great warrior. He was, however, half human and not immortal like his mother was. He would someday become old and die, and he also could be killed.

Helen of Troy in the Ephesus Museum

THE TROJAN WAR

Once Helen, who was married to Menelaus, the Greek King, was captured by Paris, the Trojan Prince, the Greeks went to battle for her safe return. Achilles joined in this war and brought a group of forceful soldiers along, known as the Myrmidons.

During this war, he was unstoppable and killed many of Troy's best warriors. The battle, however, raged on for many years. Several of the Greek gods were also involved, with some of them assisting the Greeks and some helping the Trojans.

Tojan War

Briseis and Achilles

Achilles at one point during the war captured Briseis, a beautiful princess, and fell in love. Agamemnon, the leader of the Greek Army, however, became angry at Achilles and took her away from him. Achilles then became depressed and would not fight any longer.

Since Achilles was no longer fighting, the Greeks started losing this battle. Hector was the strongest warrior of Troy, and no one was able to stop him. Patroclus, a soldier, was Achilles' best friend and convinced Achilles to let him use his armor and entered the war dressed like Achilles. Believing that Achilles had returned, the Greek army became inspired and started to fight harder.

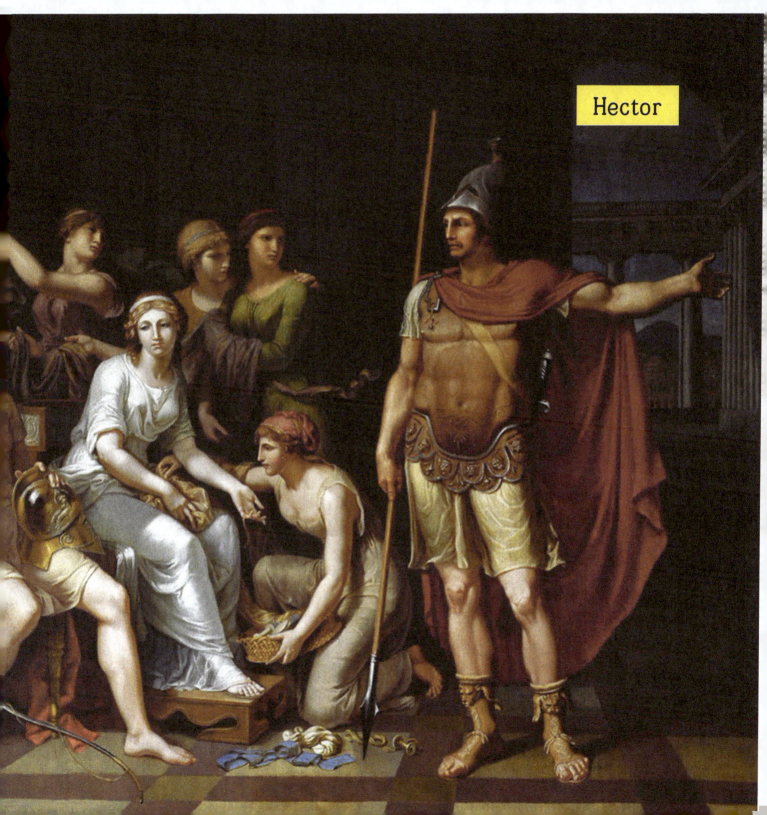

Patroclus

Just as things started to improve for the Greeks, Patroclus met Hector and the two engaged in a battle. Along with assistance from the god Apollo, Hector managed to kill Patroclus and retrieved the armor that had been borrowed from Achilles. Achilles then joined in the battle once again to avenge the death of his friend. He would meet up with Hector and, after a long battle, would defeat him.

DEATH

He would continue battle with the Trojans and it seemed as if he could not be killed. The Greek god, Apollo, however, knew his weakness. As Paris of Troy shot an arrow towards Achilles, Apollo helped guide it towards Achilles' heel and eventually, Achilles would die from this wound.

Paris Kills Achilles

Achilles Heel

THE ACHILLES' HEEL

Today, the phrase "Achilles' heel" is used when describing a point of weakness that could possible lead to someone's downfall.

FEMALE DEMIGODS

There were also three famous female demigods, referred to as demigoddesses. They are Helen of Troy, Harmonia and Clymene. Helen of Troy was the beautiful daughter of Zeus and Leda, who was Tyndareus's wife. Tyndareus was the King of Sparta. Clymene was the daughter of Tethys and Oceanus (Titan gods), and the mother parent of Prometheus and Atlas. Harmonia was the daughter of Electra and Zeus and the wife of Cadmus. The gods turned her into a serpent.

Helen of Troy

Rage of Achilles

There are many more Greek demigods from Greek mythology, each with their own intriguing story. Greek mythology is fun and amazing to learn about because of the different people, creatures, and legends to read about.

For additional information about these demigods and other characters that are part of Greek mythology, you can go to your local library, research the internet, and ask questions of your teachers, family and friends.

Printed in the USA
CPSIA information can be obtained
at www.ICGtesting.com
LVHW080733261024
794881LV00014B/710